Your Body for Life

Nutrition

From birth to old age

Robert Snedden

Heinemann
LIBRARY
Chicago, Illinois

Edited by Andrew Farrow, Adam Miller, and Adrian Vigliano

Designed by Cynthia Della-Rovere

Original illustrations © Capstone Global Library Ltd.

Illustrated by HL Studios Ltd.

Picture research by Mica Brancic

Production by Victoria Fitzgerald

Originated by Capstone Global Library Ltd.

Printed and bound in China by Leo Paper Products Ltd.

16 15 14 13 12

10 9 8 7 6 5 4 3 2 1

Library of Congress Cataloging-in-Publication Data

Snedden, Robert.

 Nutrition : from birth to old age / Robert Snedden.

    p. cm.—(Your body for life)

Includes bibliographical references and index.

 ISBN 978-1-4329-7086-4 (hb)—ISBN 978-1-4329-7093-2 (pb)
1. Nutrition. 2. Human body. I. Title.

RA784.S599 2013

613.2—dc23   2012014551

Acknowledgments

The author and publishers are grateful to the following for permission to reproduce copyright material: Alamy pp. 8 (© Nic Cleave), 9 (© Gallo Images/2A Images), 10 (© Picture Partners), 28 (© Fancy/FancyVeerSet12), 32 (© Mark Bassett), 39 (© PHOTOTAKE Inc./Kevin A Somerville), 43 (© WoodyStock), 45 (© David J. Green), 55 (© David Taylor), 53 (© Panorama media); Corbis pp. 4 (Blend Images/© Hill Street Studios), 11 (Blend Images/© Ariel Skelley), 12 (© Karen Kasmauski), 18 (© Dex Image), 19 (© moodboard), 21 (© Owen Franken), 24 (© Radius Images), 37 (Design Pics/© Ron Nickel), 47 (© Robert Michael); Science Photo Library p. 49 (Paseika); Shutterstock pp. 14 (© Marcel Jancovic), 17 (© Anneka), 23 (© Arthur Ng Heng Kui), 30 (© Aaron Amat), 34 (© Rido), 36 (© Julian Chen), 40 (© Picsfive), 41 (© Africa Studio), 41 (© Africa Studio), 41 (© Alexander Raths), 41 (© Chimpinski), 41 (© Effe45), 41 (© Marek H.), 41 (© Monticello), 41 (© ULKASTUDIO), 41 (© Valzan), 41 (© Viktar Malyshchyts), 41 (© Volosina), 50 (© Monkey Business Images).

Cover photograph of assorted seafood reproduced with permission of Shutterstock (© shadow216).

We would like to thank David Wright for his invaluable help in the preparation of this book.

Every effort has been made to contact copyright holders of any material reproduced in this book. Any omissions will be rectified in subsequent printings if notice is given to the publisher.

Disclaimer

Contents

Some words are printed in **bold**, like this. You can find out what they mean by looking in the glossary on page 60.

The Food We Eat

From the time we first develop in the womb until the day we die, our bodies are always active. Even when we are asleep, our body systems are in constant operation. Our hearts beat continually, we keep breathing, our **digestive system** and **nervous system** are at work, and our body **cells** are repaired and renewed. All of this activity requires a supply of energy and a source of raw materials. Both of these things come from the food we eat.

Food for all
Food plays an important part in our lives, not just for nutrition but also as something we can share and enjoy with other people.

What is nutrition?

Nutrition is the science of food. The substances in food that the body needs for all its activities—such as growth, repair, movement, and the senses—are called **nutrients**. Nutrition involves studying the nutrients found in different foods and how the body makes use of them, so that we can stay active and healthy.

Digestion

It is the job of the digestive system to process the food we eat and make the nutrients it contains available to the body. Digestion starts with chewing, and it continues in the stomach and intestines. There, the food is broken down into fragments small enough to be absorbed into the bloodstream from the intestines and transported to the body's cells. The process of digestion requires energy, too, just like all other body activities. After we have swallowed our food, we take no conscious part in digestion until we reach the process of egestion, which is when we go to the bathroom to get rid of the undigested leftovers of our food.

Types of nutrients	Examples
Macronutrients (type of nutrient needed in relatively large amounts)	**Carbohydrates** (provide energy and **fiber**, if whole grain) **Proteins** (used to build and repair body **tissues**; help to fight infection; provide energy) **Fats** (provide energy)
Micronutrients (type of nutrient needed in small quantities)	**Vitamins** (substances needed in tiny amounts by the body for normal growth and activity) Vitamin A (helps keep skin healthy; promotes growth) B vitamins (help the body convert food "fuel" into energy) Vitamin B1 (helps keep **nerves** healthy) Vitamin B2 (helps keep eyes healthy) Vitamin B9 (**folic acid**, or folate) and vitamin B12 (help in producing red blood cells and in the function of the nervous system) Vitamin C (involved in the growth and repair of body tissues, it helps form skin, tendons, ligaments, and blood vessels) Vitamin D (helps the body build strong teeth and bones) Vitamin E (helps maintain nerves and blood vessels)
Macrominerals (substances needed by the body in fairly large amounts)	Calcium (needed for strong teeth and bones) Magnesium (needed for muscles and nerves to work properly; helps the body use carbohydrates, proteins, and fats) Sodium, chloride, and potassium (these **minerals** work together to regulate the nervous system, muscle function, and the absorption of nutrients by the body)
Microminerals (substances needed by the body in small amounts)	Iron (an essential component of red blood cells) Zinc (essential for growth and maintenance and for healing wounds) Manganese (needed for bone development and other body tissues)
Water	Water is absolutely essential for life—all of the chemical reactions in cells take place in water. As part of the blood, it transports nutrients and substances around the body. Two-thirds of your body weight is water. (See pages 34-35.)

Calories

You have probably noticed that, among other things, packaging tells you how many **calories** a food has. Calories are a measure of how much energy there is in food. A calorie is equal to 4.184 joules. Confusingly, although food energy is often referred to simply as calories, these values are actually **kilocalories**. A kilocalorie is 1,000 calories. It is the energy needed to raise the temperature of 1 kilogram of water by 1 degree Celsius.

Everything you do uses up calories. Many different **chemical reactions** take place in the body as energy and nutrients are used. This is called **metabolism**.

What's on your plate?

When we sit down to eat, we are probably not looking at what is in front of us in terms of **macronutrients** and **micronutrients**. We are much more interested in flavor and aroma (smell)! But it is important that we give some thought to what is in the food we eat. We should aim to have a balanced diet—one that will provide all the nutrients we need, and in the right proportions, for good health.

Health authorities in different countries have issued guidelines on the proportions of each food type we should eat for a healthy diet. These may be shown in a graphical form such as the Eatwell Plate designed by the Food Standards Agency in the United Kingdom and MyPlate produced by the United States Department of Agriculture. The purpose of these guidelines is to encourage people to think about what they are putting on their plates in terms of good nutrition.

Food groups

All of the foods we eat can be divided into five major food groups:

- fruits and vegetables
- starchy foods—rice, pasta, bread, and potatoes (sources of **carbohydrates**)
- meat, fish, eggs, and beans (sources of protein)
- milk and dairy products
- fats and sugars

Keeping in proportion

This food plate shows the proportion of each food group we should be eating. The detail of guidelines might vary from country to country, but the basic proportions are good advice for most people.

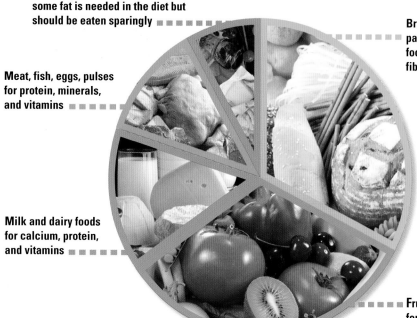

Food and drinks high in fat/sugar—some fat is needed in the diet but should be eaten sparingly

Meat, fish, eggs, pulses for protein, minerals, and vitamins

Bread, rice, potatoes, pasta, and other starchy foods for carbohydrates, fiber, and vitamins

Milk and dairy foods for calcium, protein, and vitamins

Fruit and vegetables for vitamins, minerals, and fiber

Food labeling

In many countries, including the United States, packaged foods have a label that tells us what is contained in the food. This nutrition information label should list all of the ingredients in the product, ordered according to the amount of each one in the food. It should say how much the food provides in terms of carbohydrates, proteins, fats, salt, sugar, and so on. These details can help with planning a healthy, balanced diet.

Appetite and appestat

Many things can affect our appetite. One of the most obvious reasons for eating is hunger. Our empty stomachs grumble and send signals to the brain, prompting us to find food.

The part of the brain that controls our appetite is called the **appestat**. An empty stomach, low blood sugar, low temperatures, and even the hours of daylight can all trigger the appestat, making us feel hungry and in need of something to eat. Regular exercise appears to play a role in helping the appestat link the body's calorie intake to its energy requirements. But there is more to appetite than just a simple need to supply the body with energy. Our moods and emotions also have an effect on our eating behavior. The smell, sight, or taste of something we find delicious can stimulate the desire to eat, whether or not we are actually hungry.

Life stages

At different stages in our lives, we will need different things from our diets. For example, young children are growing and developing rapidly, and so they need a diet that is high in nutrients—particularly proteins for building new body tissues—and that provides a good source of energy. The digestive system gets less efficient at moving food along as we get older, so older people can benefit from a diet high in fiber, which assists the passage of food through the digestive system.

AMAZING BUT TRUE!

Slow response

From the time we start eating, it can take 20 minutes for the amount of sugar in the blood to rise high enough to turn off the brain's appestat switch. That's plenty of time to pack away a few hundred more calories than we actually need! Keep that in mind and remind yourself to slow down while eating to give your brain time to catch up.

Baby Building

Nutrition is very important during pregnancy. It is the major factor that affects the growth and development of the **fetus** in the womb. The food a pregnant woman eats can have an effect not only on her own health, but also on that of her developing baby.

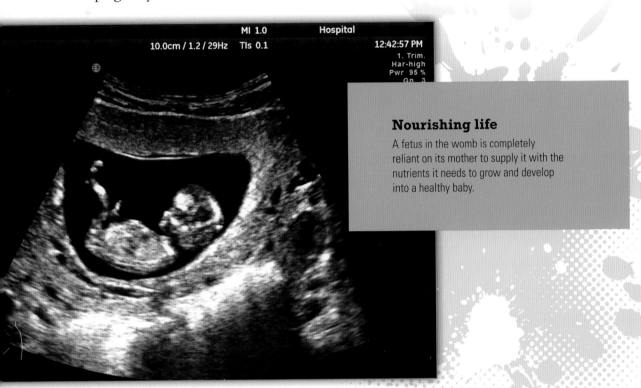

MI 1.0   Hospital
10.0cm / 1.2 / 29Hz   Tls 0.1   12:42:57 PM
1. Trim.
Har-high
Pwr 95 %
Gn 3

Nourishing life

A fetus in the womb is completely reliant on its mother to supply it with the nutrients it needs to grow and develop into a healthy baby.

Eating for two?

You might imagine that a pregnant woman would need extra calories in her diet to provide the energy used in the growth of the child. But when researchers carried out careful measurements of the amount of food being eaten by pregnant women in **developed countries**, they discovered that they were not eating much more than women who were not pregnant.

From three months into the pregnancy until birth, the woman's daily energy requirements increase by around 300 calories a day. A lot of the extra energy needed for the growth of the fetus comes from a combination of more efficient metabolism and a decrease in the amount of exercise pregnant women get.

But there is more of a need to increase the amount of food eaten during pregnancy when the woman's food intake is barely adequate to begin with. This may often be the case in **developing countries**.

Extra requirements

During pregnancy, women should increase the amount of some nutrients in the diet. The requirements for iron and folic acid (vitamin B9) double, for example. Folic acid is very important for the proper development of the brain and spinal cord. Much of this can be made up through the diet—peas, beans, and whole-grain cereals are good sources of folic acid. Some doctors will also advise taking **supplements**, to ensure an adequate supply. However, taking multivitamin supplements is not a good idea during pregnancy. Too much vitamin A, for example, can lead to problems with the growth and development of the fetus.

Nutrition for two

Taking care to ensure a balanced and nutritious diet helps to maintain the health of mother and baby during pregnancy.

AMAZING BUT TRUE!

Cravings

You might have heard stories about pregnant women eating strange things, like lumps of dirt or chalk. This craving for substances with little or no nutritional value is called pica. The reason why this happens to some women is not certain. Some researchers think it may be connected to a lack of vitamins and minerals in the diet, such as an iron **deficiency**. There is a danger that some of the substances eaten may be poisonous and cause harm.

Weight gain in pregnancy

The amount of weight gained by women during pregnancy varies enormously, from about 13 pounds (6 kilograms) to 53 pounds (24 kilograms). There appears to be a relationship between the mother's weight gain and the birth weight of the child. A number of studies have shown an increase in birth weight of around 0.6 to 0.8 ounce (17 to 23 grams) for every kilogram (which is over 2 pounds) gained by the mother.

In developing countries, where nutrition may be poor, mothers gain little weight during pregnancy. This is because of their restricted diet and because they may also have to carry out physical work. As a consequence, birth weights in developing countries are lower than those in developed countries.

Milk

Mammals are unique in the animal world because adult females can produce milk to feed their young. Humans are a type of mammal, and human mothers have been breast-feeding their children for as long as humans have existed. It is only since the 1860s that formula milk, derived from cow's milk, has been available as an alternative.

First food

For the first few months of life, all of a baby's nutritional needs are met by just one type of food—milk. This can be either breast milk or a substitute made from cow's milk, with nutrients added to make it closer to human milk.

The breast-feeding mother has increased requirements for a number of nutrients, including vitamin A, vitamin D, vitamin C, B vitamins (particularly folic acid), and a number of minerals, including calcium, phosphorus, and magnesium. A varied and balanced diet will ensure an adequate supply of almost all of these nutrients.

The only vitamin that might not be present in adequate amounts in breast milk is vitamin D. In some countries, doctors recommend a daily supplement of vitamin D for as long as breast-feeding is continued. In the United States, it is given to the child, while in some other places, including the United Kingdom, the mother takes the supplement. Both methods appear to be effective.

Mother's milk
Breast milk provides all the nutrition a baby needs during the first few months of its life.

Making a choice

Although health care professionals may offer advice—the World Health Organization recommends that babies are breast-fed exclusively for the first half of infancy, for example—the decision about how to feed a baby belongs to the mother. Many will choose breast-feeding as the more natural thing to do, but some will opt for bottle-feeding from the beginning. Solids should be introduced at around six months, with breast or bottle-feeding continuing as the amounts of other foods are gradually increased.

The advantages of breast-feeding

There is a great deal of scientific evidence to support the idea that breast-feeding reduces the risk of illnesses such as diarrhea and respiratory (breathing) infections in both mother and baby. Importantly, components found in breast milk produced in the first few days after birth also help to protect the baby from bacteria and other harmful infections.

Some studies have shown that children who have been breast-fed are at a lower risk of becoming **obese** later in childhood and are less likely to have high blood pressure as adults. Breast-feeding has been particularly associated with lower levels of **cholesterol** in later life, which can reduce the chances of heart disease.

The case for formula feeding

Breast-feeding is not for everyone. Some women may find it difficult or stressful to breast-feed, or there may be medical reasons why they cannot do so. Commercially prepared milk formulas are an adequate alternative to breast milk and may actually contain higher concentrations of nutrients. However, there is evidence that some nutrients, such as iron and zinc, are better absorbed from breast milk than formula milk.

Share the care

One advantage of using formula milk in place of, or alongside, breast milk is that it allows the father to share in feeding the baby, too!

Lifelong consequences

Nutrition is of vital importance from the start of life. There is evidence that inadequate nutrition, resulting in poor growth in the womb and during the first two years of life, can have an effect on the way a person develops in later life. A poor diet in the first two years can mean that a person will do less well in school and be shorter as an adult.

Malnutrition and development

Malnutrition is one of the world's biggest health problems. Malnutrition does not simply mean not having enough to eat. It means a diet that lacks the essential nutrients for growth and development. Recent research has linked malnutrition in the first years of life with behavioral problems in later years.

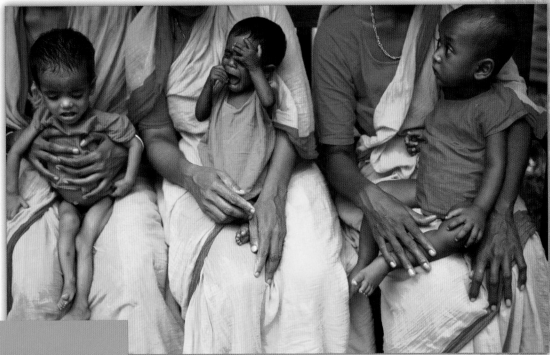

Early days matter

Lack of adequate nutrition for growing children can be a particular concern for children in less economically developed countries as it can lead to health problems in later life.

Nutrients such as zinc, iron, and vitamin B are all linked with brain development. If these are lacking in a child's diet, this may lead to lower intelligence and antisocial behavior in later life. For 14 years, researchers monitored the development of children on the Indian Ocean island of Mauritius. They found that those children who showed signs of being malnourished at age three were 51 percent more likely to show violent and antisocial behavior at age 17.

The first thousand days

Researchers have been discovering the vital role played by nutrition during the first 1,000 days of development—or from conception until around the second birthday.

In the 1980s, Professor David Barker noticed that areas in England and Wales where there had been child health problems also had high rates of heart disease about 60 years later. With a team from the United Kingdom's Medical Research Council, he compared thousands of people's birth details with their adult medical histories. He discovered that boys who had a low birth weight were at much higher risk of developing heart disease as adults. In girls, low birth weight was also linked to the risk of **stroke** in later life. As the research continued, more links were discovered between early

The 1,000 Days partnership

The 1,000 Days partnership was launched in 2010 with a goal of improving nutrition worldwide across the crucial first 1,000 days of development. Organizations such as Actionaid, UNICEF, Child Fund International, and the International Medical Corps are all 1,000 Days partners.

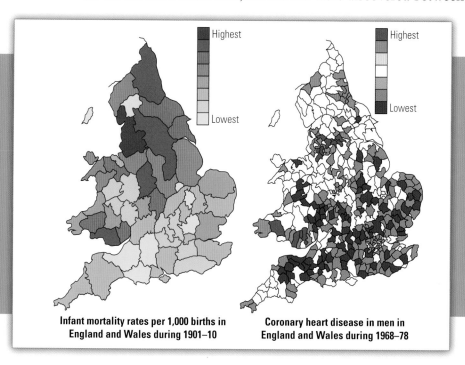

Infant mortality rates per 1,000 births in England and Wales during 1901–10

Coronary heart disease in men in England and Wales during 1968–78

Learning from the past

Professor David Barker noticed a remarkable similarity between a map showing infant mortality at the beginning of the 20th century and another showing incidences of heart disease about 60 years later. It led him to put forward a theory that health in childhood could have an effect on adult health.

nutrition and adult health. Babies with low birth weight were more likely to suffer from chronic bronchitis, a respiratory illness, because a lack of nutrients meant their lungs did not develop properly. They might also have problems with high blood pressure.

Based on these findings, Barker suggested that there are key windows of development in a child's early life. Poor nutrition at any of these crucial stages results in weaknesses being built into the growing person. It is these weaknesses that make the person more likely to develop illness in later life.

Childhood

The early years of childhood are important nutritionally, not only because the child is growing and developing rapidly, but also because patterns of eating can be established at this time that may carry over into adult life.

Weaning

Weaning is the stage of development when a child begins to move from an exclusively milk diet to one that includes other foods. There are several indications that show the child is ready for weaning:

- doubling of the birth weight
- good control of the head and neck
- the ability to sit up with some support
- indicating having had enough to eat by turning the head away or not opening the mouth
- beginning to show an interest in the food others are eating

Most babies should start a mixed diet between four and six months old. By this age, milk, whether from the breast or the bottle, will be inadequate for the child's needs for nutrients such as iron, zinc, and vitamin C.

New sensations

Babies often make faces when trying new foods, and may even spit the new food out, but this doesn't necessarily mean they are unhappy. This is just a normal reaction to experiencing new sensations and tasting new flavors.

Solid food timeline Every baby is different, but, in general, the progression from a milk-only diet to a diet of regular food will be along these lines:	**1–4 months**	**4–6 months**	**6–7 months**
	Breast or formula milk only	Small amounts of cereal added to the milk	Mashed fruits and vegetables

The first food offered may be a thin paste of iron-enriched infant rice cereal mixed with breast milk or formula. After this, a variety of foods can be tried, such as mashed potatoes, oatmeal, and mashed fruits. Solid foods should be introduced one ingredient at a time, spaced over a few days, so that **allergies** or food **intolerances** (see pages 20 and 21) can be spotted. The child should be given foods from each of the major food groups—cereals, fruits and vegetables, meat and fish, and dairy products. However, it best to avoid combinations of foods until it is certain that there are no intolerances to worry about.

The second six months

During the second six months, the child can be introduced to liquids others than milk, such as fruit juices. Untreated cow's milk is not recommended for children under a year old, however, because it may cause irritation and bleeding in the digestive tract. This problem does not occur with boiled milk or the treated milk used in formula. Gradually, chewier foods like bread, cheese, and pieces of apple can be brought into the diet.

Milk will still be the main source of calories, but it should gradually become less important. The most important nutrients for growth and development at this stage are protein and iron, both of which can be found in foods such as finely ground beef and in peas and beans. Salt and sugar should not be added to an infant's diet. Too much salt can damage the baby's developing kidneys, and a dependency on sugar could lead to childhood **obesity**.

AMAZING BUT TRUE!

Hold the salt

A breast-fed infant gets just one twentieth of the salt found in the diet of a typical adult in a developed country.

8–9 months	9 months	10 months	12 months
Soft finger foods, such as pieces of banana	Meats and citrus fruit juice (drunk from a cup, not a bottle)	Cooked egg yolks and bite-sized foods	Most regular foods can be offered, but not small, hard foods like nuts that may cause choking

Early years

The first few years of childhood, between weaning and starting school, are a time when children begin to develop their own tastes. The rapid growth that has taken place during the first year begins to slow, and young children can become less interested in eating.

Taste perceptions

Infants appear to be born able to distinguish between sweet and bitter, but the ability to detect other tastes, such as saltiness, does not develop until around six months old. A young child's taste perceptions are different from those of an adult. Young children dislike things that taste bitter, and they prefer sweeter foods. The reasons for this can be traced back to early humans foraging for foods such as fruits and berries. Sweet-tasting foods are high in energy, while foods that taste bitter may be poisonous.

First foods

The first food given to an infant differs from one culture to another. In the Western world, infants often start with commercially prepared baby cereals, going on to prepared foods like mashed fruits and vegetables packaged in jars. In China and other Asian countries, it is much more common to prepare foods at home. Babies are often given a mashed rice porridge called xifan. In West Africa, a maize (corn) porridge may be a child's first solid food. In many parts of the world, including Southeast Asia and sub-Saharan Africa, it is common for the caregiver to chew the food before passing it to the infant. It is probably a fairly common practice in developing countries, too.

Infant needs

Young children may be small, but because they are growing and developing they have high energy and nutrient requirements for their size. Because young children will eat smaller amounts than older children it is important that they have regular meals that provide the energy and nutrients they need. The low-fat, high-fiber diet that is recommended for older children and adults is not suitable for young children, particularly those below the age of two, as it may not provide sufficient energy, fat, iron, or zinc, and is likely to be too high in fiber for this age. From around the ages of two to five, children can gradually be introduced to a diet that is more in line with the healthy adult diet, which should have more fiber and less reliance on fat as an energy source.

I don't want that!

As children grow older they are more likely to try to make their own choices about what they want to eat, but this might lead to tantrums at meal times!

Fussy eaters

Between the ages of around one to three years old, some children go through a phase of refusing foods they had previously enjoyed and being generally less enthusiastic about eating. One reason for this change in behavior is that the rate of growth has slowed down. The speed with which weight increases may be only a quarter of what it was previously. Height increases will have slowed by a half.

There is also the fact that children are growing in awareness at this time. They are discovering that they are independent and are beginning to make their own choices. Parents and caregivers have to adopt a variety of tactics to deal with this behavior, such as getting the child to eat bread and to drink fruit juices to substitute for the fiber and vitamins found in fresh vegetables.

Calorie requirements

The number of calories we need to consume per day changes according to our age and how active we are.

Gender	Age	Sedentary (not active)	Moderately Active	Active
Male or female	2-3	1,000	1,000-1,400	1,000-1,400
Female	4–8	1,200	1,400–1,600	1,400–1,800
	9–13	1,600	1,600–2,000	1,800–2,200
	14–18	1,800	2,000	2,400
	19–30	2,000	2,000–2,200	2,400
	31–50	1,800	2,000	2,200
	51+	1,600	1,800	2,200
Male	4–8	1,400	1,400–1,600	1,600–2,000
	9–13	1,800	1,800–2,200	2,000–2,600
	14–18	2,200	2,400–2,800	2,800–3,200
	19–30	2,400	2,600–2,800	3,000
	31–50	2,200	2,400–2,600	2,800–3,000
	51+	2,000	2,200–2,400	2,400–2,800

School days

When children reach school age, they are still growing and developing rapidly, and it is important that they continue to eat foods that are rich in nutrients. However, as they begin to spend more time away from home, their diets are no longer completely under the control of parents or guardians.

A healthy start
Many nutritionists think that a healthy breakfast is the most important meal of the day—not just for children, but for all of us—as it provides energy and nutrition for the day ahead.

The challenge of obesity

One of the major concerns regarding nutrition in schoolchildren is the rising problem of obesity. According to figures published in the United States, the percentage of children between the ages of 6 and 11 who were obese went up from 7 percent in 1980 to nearly 20 percent (1 in 5) in 2008. These numbers appear set to increase. Being overweight is a major issue because it can lead to health problems such as heart disease.

Nutrition and learning

We have seen how nutrient deficiencies can lead to behavioral problems (see page 12). Research has also found links between nutrients and learning. A study carried out in Australia and Indonesia showed that children who were regularly given a drink containing a number of micronutrients did better on tests of verbal learning skills and memory than children who were not given the drink.

How do we gain weight?

As we saw earlier, all of the chemical reactions going on in the cells of the body make up its metabolism (see page 5). The amount of energy the body uses over a period of time is called the **metabolic rate**. This rate is not the same for everyone, and it depends on things like age, body size, and how active we are.

The energy intake from food and the energy used up by metabolism need to be kept in balance for good health. If the amount of food we eat is more than we need for metabolism, the body simply stores the excess away as fat and we gain weight. If the food we are eating does not supply enough energy, the body will use up its fat stores to make up the shortfall and we lose weight. In extreme cases of malnutrition, the body breaks down muscle tissue to provide the energy needed.

Exercise and dieting

In developed countries, children are using less energy than ever before, because they are driven to school and, in some cases, participate less in sports and physical activities. They do not burn off extra calories. For this reason, many children in developed countries are obese.

Several studies have shown the importance of physical activity in controlling weight. Exercising can help reduce body fat levels without losing muscle mass. In fact, exercise will increase muscle mass, which means an increase in the metabolic rate.

Sometimes people "diet" to lose weight. But simply reducing calorie intake by dieting leads to a loss of muscle mass and body water. When the body loses muscle mass, its metabolic rate decreases, and it becomes less able to burn calories. If the person then comes off the low-calorie diet and energy intake increases again, fat is regained more easily than before.

Storing up trouble

Obesity is increasingly becoming a problem in developed countries. It is easy for people who get little exercise and who consume too many high calorie, low nutrient foods to become overweight.

Food allergies

The body's **immune system** is its first line of defense against invasion by bacteria, viruses, and other substances that could harm us. Sometimes, however, the immune system defends the body against substances that are actually harmless. These can include pollen or dust, resulting in the sneezing and watery eyes of hay fever. This type of oversensitive reaction of the immune system is called an allergy. Many people—including children—can also be allergic to certain foods, sometimes with life-threatening consequences.

Eight types of food are responsible for most food allergies. Eggs, milk, soy, and wheat mostly affect children, while shellfish (for example, crab and shrimp) and nuts (for example, walnuts, almonds, and Brazil nuts) affect adults. Both children and adults can be allergic to peanuts.

AMAZING BUT TRUE!

Amazing allergy facts

- More than 170 foods have been found to cause allergies.
- More than 3 percent of adults have one or more food allergies.
- Children with a food allergy are two to four times more likely to have other allergies and asthma (a condition that causes difficulty with breathing).
- About 6.5 million Americans are allergic to seafood.
- Milk allergy is the most common childhood food allergy.
- Food allergies cause approximately 150 to 200 deaths each year in the United States.

Allergy versus intolerance		
This chart shows some of the basic differences between food allergies and intolerances.		
	Allergy	**Intolerance**
Sensitivity	Just a tiny particle of food can be enough to trigger an allergic reaction.	A large amount of food has to be consumed to trigger an intolerance.
Symptoms	The symptoms of an allergy can appear within minutes of eating the food and can be very specific, such as a swelling of the mouth and throat.	The symptoms of a food intolerance may take several hours to appear and are more general, such as a feeling of nausea or discomfort.
Threat to life	The body's reaction to a food allergy can be severe enough to cause death.	Food intolerance can be unpleasant, but it is never a threat to life.

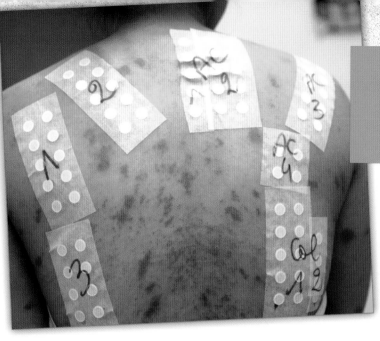

Allergies on the rise

Although food allergies or sensitivities can occur at any age, they are most common in children. In recent decades, there has been a big increase in reports of food sensitivities. A U.S. report showed that 1 out of every 25 children has a food allergy—which represents about a 20 percent increase between 1997 and 2007. There appears to be a similar trend in other countries, too.

Why food allergies are increasing so much is uncertain. One theory suggests that the decline in the amount of fruits and vegetables being eaten might be interfering with the proper development of the immune system in children. Another suggests it may be due to changes in diet. People in the Western world are eating more vegetable fats and oils and fewer animal fats, such as butter, and researchers think that the vegetable oils may be stimulating the part of the immune system that causes allergies.

To support this idea, researchers point to the fact that countries adopting a more Western diet have seen a rise in food allergies. There are also regional variations in allergies. For example, rice allergy is more of a problem in China and Japan than elsewhere, and sesame allergy is more common in Israel and the Middle East than in other areas. At present, there is no hard evidence to support these theories.

Anaphylaxis
Anaphylaxis is an extreme allergic reaction. This diagram shows the symptoms of anaphylaxis. These symptoms involve all of the major body systems, and in severe cases they may be life threatening.

Skin
(80–90% of reactions)
Hives (raised red welts), itching, flushing, swelling of lips and tongue

Brain and nervous system
(10–15% of reactions)
Headache, dizziness, feeling uneasy or confused, tunnel vision

Respiratory tract
(70% of reactions):
Tightness in throat, hoarseness, unable to speak, wheezing and tightness in the chest

Heart
(10–45% of reactions)
Chest pains, irregular heartbeat, weak pulse, dizziness and fainting

Digestive system
(30–45% of reactions)
Nausea and vomiting, abdominal cramps and pains, diarrhea

Approaching Adolescence

As children grow older, they become more responsible for deciding for themselves what they will eat. One **nutritionist** has said, "Teenagers are not fed; they eat." Of course, teenagers have much more on their minds than meal times. Their thoughts are taken up by things like schoolwork, social events, and relationships, and so missed meals and a reliance on snacks and fast foods can easily become normal.

Rapid growth

Adolescence is a time when the body is growing rapidly, as bone and muscle mass are being gained and the reproductive organs change and develop as we mature from children into adults. This means that the energy needs of a teenager are great. A 14-year-old boy may consume almost twice as many daily calories as an average adult.

It is no surprise that teenagers frequently turn to high-energy foods, which may be rich in fats and sugars, but low in nutrients. It is important that people such as parents, guardians, and schools supply teenagers with plenty of nutritious foods, such as fresh fruits and vegetables, to ensure they get all the nutrients they need to promote proper development.

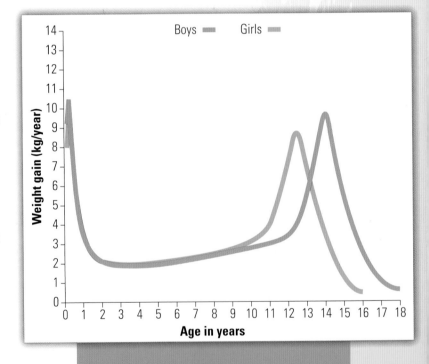

Changing rates

Children do not gain weight at a constant rate as they grow. For example, there is a marked increase at puberty (roughly age 12 for girls and 14 for boys).

Iron

Iron deficiency is a common problem among teenagers. A teenager's iron needs increase significantly throughout the period of adolescence. Girls, in particular, need to boost the amount of iron in their diet when menstruation (periods) begins, to make up for that lost in menstrual blood. Boys also need more iron in their diet because of their rapid growth and increase in blood volume. However, when growth slows, at around the age of 19, a female's iron needs are almost double that of a male.

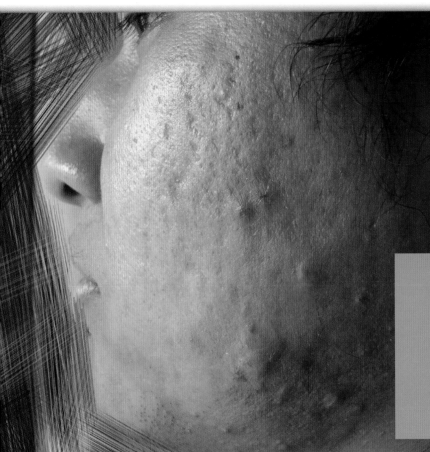

The main source of iron in the diet is red meat, but there are good meat-free alternatives such as whole wheat bread, dried fruits, and green, leafy vegetables. It is thought that vitamin C may improve the body's ability to absorb iron.

Dealing with acne

As many as 8 in 10 adolescents have the skin condition known as acne at some point. Though keeping your skin clean can be helpful in preventing acne, hormones play a major part in causing the condition. For most people, acne gets better by the time they're in their twenties.

Acne and diet

Acne is a skin condition that causes pimples to develop. It affects most people at some time in their lives and is most common among older children and **adolescents**. Many people believe that too much chocolate, fatty foods, and soft drinks can all make acne worse. Some diets even claim to cure acne. Is this true?

So far, all the research that has been carried out into the links between acne and diet has been inconclusive, and chocolate and fatty foods would appear not to be the cause. There are, of course, good dietary reasons for cutting candy and fatty foods out of the diet, beyond their possible effects on acne.

New experiences

Crossing over from childhood into adulthood is a time when many people begin to explore the variety of experiences the world has to offer. We are curious and adventurous and want to try out new things. Among these can be experimenting with new foods and drinks, including alcohol.

Alcohol

Many people try alcohol for the first time as adolescents. Teenagers may want to drink alcohol for a number of reasons. They might want to satisfy their curiosity about alcohol. They might want to fit in with their friends. They might also believe that alcohol will help them cope with stress or anxiety.

Learning about life

Teenage years are a time when young people are experimenting with new things, including some which may be harmful for them, such as alcohol.

AMAZING BUT TRUE!

Alcohol-related deaths

In the United States, around 5,000 young people under the age of 21 die each year because of alcohol-related incidents. This is nearly one-third of the number of teenagers dying from all causes each year. Alcohol-related deaths include roughly 1,900 motor vehicle crashes and 300 suicides.

The risks of drinking alcohol can be high for teenagers. Because the body is still growing and developing, it is more vulnerable to the effects of alcohol. Regular alcohol consumption has been linked to an increased risk of cancer, liver disease, heart disorders, and impotence (an inability to have sexual intercourse) in later life. Heavy drinking in adolescence may also lead to learning difficulties later on in life.

Body image

Adolescence is a time when peer pressure can play a very big part in the way we behave. It can have an important effect on teenagers' eating behavior and may lead to under-eating or overeating, as teens try to achieve an "ideal" body shape. Behavior such as extreme dieting, binge eating, and deliberately throwing up food affects more teenagers than adults, and it affects significantly more girls than boys.

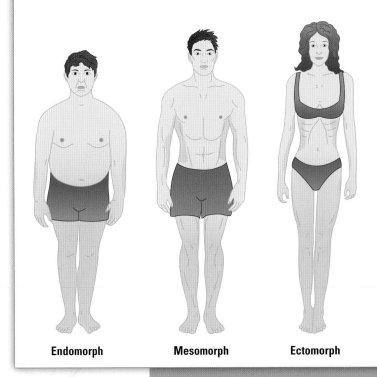

Endomorph   **Mesomorph**   **Ectomorph**

Anorexia and bulimia

Many adolescents see themselves as being too fat, while some, particularly males, think of themselves as too thin or not growing tall enough. Anorexia is an eating disorder centered on a fear of being overweight. Anorexics can become obsessed with eating and diet, and they commonly refuse to admit that there is anything wrong with their behavior. Around 5 percent of anorexics will die as a result of problems caused by malnutrition. People with bulimia try to control their body weight by eating excessive amounts (binge eating) and then deliberately making themselves vomit or using laxatives to purge themselves of food.

Research carried out in Canada found that deliberate fasting (not eating), skipping meals, and using crash diets are frequent across the country, with 22 to 46 percent of girls admitting to these practices. Between 5 and 12 percent of adolescent girls said they deliberately made themselves vomit. Similar behavior patterns have been found in many other countries, including the United States, Australia, and the United Kingdom.

Somatotypes

A person's body type is called his or her somatotype. There are three main somatotypes: endomorph (round type), mesomorph (muscular type), and ectomorph (slim type), as shown here. Your somatotype is determined by a combination of genetics (inheritance) and environment. Although people may be mostly one type or another, they will still have qualities of the other two types. A person of average build will be a balance of all three types. Sometimes people will use diet or exercise to try to give themselves a more "desirable" shape, such as the ectomorphic shape of many fashion models.

Vegetarianism

A vegetarian is someone who does not eat meat and may exclude other animal products from his or her diet as well. Many people are lifelong vegetarians because of culture and upbringing, while many others choose to become vegetarians when they begin to make food choices for themselves. Is being a vegetarian a healthy choice from a nutritional standpoint?

The advantages of vegetarianism

There is a lot of evidence to suggest that balanced vegetarian diets can offer real health advantages. Vegetarian diets have been shown to have benefits in preventing and treating conditions such as heart disease, high blood pressure, **diabetes**, kidney disease, and **osteoporosis**. A vegetarian consumes a lot less **saturated fat** and cholesterol and is likely to eat more complex carbohydrates (see page 32), dietary fiber, and vitamins C and E than a non-vegetarian.

A vegetarian plate

A vegetarian diet should be as varied as a non-vegetarian diet, the only difference being that nuts, beans, and other foods are the main sources of protein in the diet.

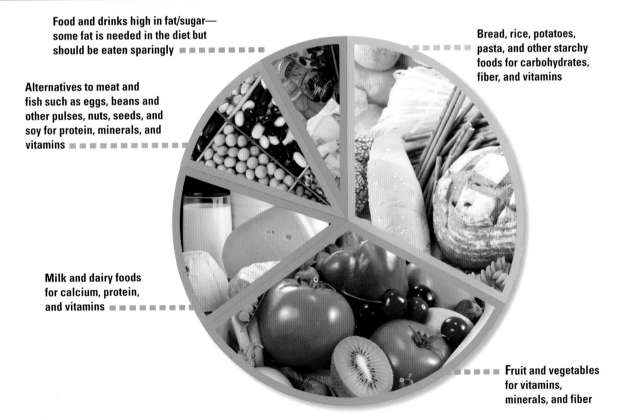

Food and drinks high in fat/sugar—some fat is needed in the diet but should be eaten sparingly ■ ■ ■ ■ ■ ■ ■ ■ ■

Bread, rice, potatoes, pasta, and other starchy foods for carbohydrates, fiber, and vitamins

Alternatives to meat and fish such as eggs, beans and other pulses, nuts, seeds, and soy for protein, minerals, and vitamins ■ ■ ■ ■ ■ ■ ■ ■ ■ ■ ■

Milk and dairy foods for calcium, protein, and vitamins ■ ■ ■ ■ ■ ■ ■ ■ ■ ■ ■

Fruit and vegetables for vitamins, minerals, and fiber

Vegetarian tradition

People belonging to cultures with a long tradition of vegetarianism have healthy diets that supply all the nutrients they need. They have a good intake of protein, for example, from meals that include a variety of peas, beans, and nuts.

But people who decide to become vegetarian as part of a lifestyle choice may have an inadequate diet if they do no more than simply remove meat from their plates. They need to adjust their intake of other foods to make up for the missing nutrients. Good meal planning is essential to ensure a healthy, nutritious diet. (And of course this is true for everyone else as well, not just vegetarians.) A well-balanced vegetarian diet is suitable for everyone, from professional athletes to young children and the elderly.

Veganism

Veganism is the strictest form of vegetarianism, and it allows no animal products in the diet at all. Vegans do not have access to the best sources of calcium—for example, they do not eat dairy products like milk and cheese—and they must obtain calcium from other sources, such as broccoli and soy.

Vegans can also run the risk of being deficient in vitamin B12. Vitamin B12 is not found naturally in any plant foods, although it is often added to cereals along with other vitamins and nutrients (adding nutrients to a food is called fortifying). Vitamin B12 is involved in the formation of red blood cells and in the functioning of the nervous system. In 2003, German researchers reported that 92 percent of the vegans they studied were deficient in vitamin B12. Supplements of B12 are essential for the infants of vegans and for vegan women during pregnancy.

Types of vegetarianism

There are different degrees of vegetarian diets, with varying restrictions on what can be eaten:

- Pescatarians do not eat meat, but they will eat fish, eggs, and dairy products. Strictly speaking, this is not a vegetarian diet.

- Lacto-ovo vegetarians do not eat meat or fish, but they will eat milk and eggs. This is the most common type of vegetarianism.

- Lacto-vegetarians do not eat meat, fish, or eggs, but they will eat dairy products.

- Vegans do not eat any animal products at all.

Into Adulthood:
The Prime of Life

The period from our twenties to our forties is generally when we are at our fittest and healthiest. Our bodies are fully developed and have not yet begun the inevitable decline into old age. It is also a time when we have the most control over the lives we lead and the food we eat.

Staying healthy

Even though our bodies have stopped growing and developing, our cells are continually being repaired and renewed throughout life, so a healthy diet is just as important for adults as it is for children. Many of the risk factors for illness are diet-related and may be the result of habits picked up during adolescence. Among these may be eating too many foods that are rich in fats and sugars, which leads to obesity; eating a diet too high in salt, which leads to raised blood pressure (see page 31); and drinking too much alcohol, which leads to a variety of risks (see page 29).

For many people, it can be all too easy to grab a snack rather than take the time to prepare a nourishing meal. It can also be easy to slip into the habit of reaching for alcohol to unwind at the end of the day.

Busy, busy
Adulthood is a fast-paced, high energy time for many people. Learning to maintain a balanced diet despite the demands of a busy lifestyle is an important challenge for everyone.

Empty calories

Foods with "empty calories" are those that are high in calories and low in nutrients. These are generally foods that are high in saturated fats and/or sugars. Common empty calorie foods are cakes, pastries, ice cream, hot dogs, fries, chips, and soft drinks. When men become overweight, they tend to build up extra fat around the abdominal area. (Women are more likely to store fat on their hips and thighs.) Extra abdominal fat puts strain on body organs, increasing the risk of developing heart disease and diabetes.

Alcohol

Anyone who drinks alcohol excessively risks damaging their health. Regularly drinking too much alcohol can lead to irreversible liver damage over a period of time. Binge drinking may increase blood pressure and raise the risk of an eventual heart attack.

The risks for women may be greater than they are for men. Women have less body water than men. This means that if a man and woman of the same weight drink the same amount of alcohol, the woman's blood alcohol concentration will be higher. Women drinkers are more likely to develop liver and heart problems than men who drink a similar amount. Women who drink two to five alcoholic drinks a day increase their chances of developing breast cancer by about one and a half times the chances of women who do not drink.

Researchers have found a link between moderate consumption of alcohol and a reduction in the risk of heart disease. The relationship between the two is unclear, although alcohol appears to play a part in reducing the risk of blood clots forming. However, the dangers of drinking too much alcohol far outweigh these potential benefits.

A danger to others

Excess alcohol consumption can be a danger to others, too. This map shows rates of self-reported alcohol-impaired driving episodes among adults in the United States in 2010.

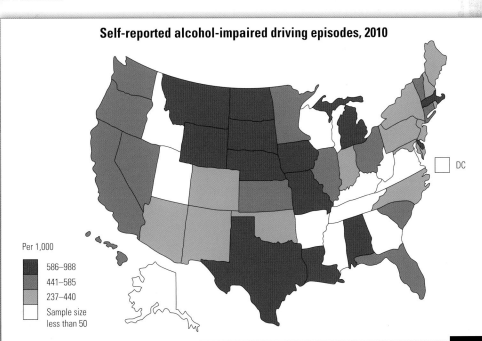

Self-reported alcohol-impaired driving episodes, 2010

DC

Per 1,000

- 586–988
- 441–585
- 237–440
- Sample size less than 50

29

The salt solution

We need to have some salt (sodium chloride) in our diet. The human body needs a small amount of sodium to contract and relax muscles, for the nervous system to work properly, and to maintain the proper balance of water and minerals.

However, too much salt in the diet has been linked to conditions such as high blood pressure in adults. Also, as mentioned earlier (see page 15), it is dangerous in babies, because their underdeveloped kidneys cannot cope with large amounts of salt.

Over-salted?

Doctors recommend that healthy adults limit their intake of salt to no more than 6 grams a day. (In people over the age of 40, or with a condition such as high blood pressure or diabetes, this falls to less than 4 grams a day.) But the current intake in Western countries is closer to 9 grams per day. A report published by the U.S. Institute of Medicine estimates that 100,000 lives a year could be saved in the United States if sodium intake were reduced to the levels recommended.

Know your diet

Think about your diet. How salty are the foods you typically eat? How much salt do you add to your food? How many processed and prepared foods do you eat as opposed to fresh, homemade meals? These are all important questions to ask as you begin to consider your salt intake.

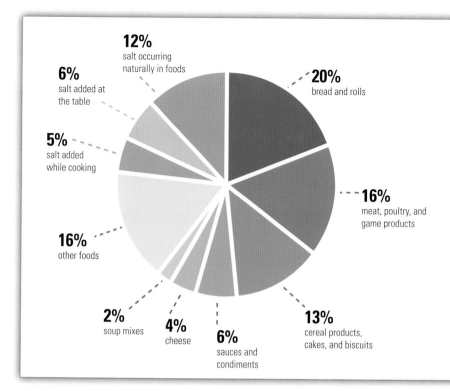

12%
salt occurring
naturally in foods

6%
salt added at
the table

5%
salt added
while cooking

16%
other foods

2%
soup mixes

4%
cheese

6%
sauces and
condiments

13%
cereal products,
cakes, and biscuits

20%
bread and rolls

16%
meat, poultry, and
game products

Sources of salt
Most of the salt consumed
by people in the world's
developed countries comes
from processed foods.

High-salt foods

Everyone knows that chips and "junk food" can be very salty. You might not realize it, but the following foods are also almost always high in salt. To cut down on salt, you should eat the following foods less often or in smaller amounts:

- bacon
- cheese
- ham
- olives
- pickles
- salami
- salted and dry roasted nuts
- smoked meat and fish
- soy sauce

Other prepared foods, such as canned soups and bottled sauces, can vary greatly in their salt content. This is where food labeling can be invaluable in helping to make healthy choices.

Where the salt comes from

In developed countries, it can be difficult to control the amount of salt in the diet—over three-quarters of the salt we consume is already in the food most people eat, such as bread, breakfast cereals, and prepared foods, since it is added as a flavor enhancer. Checking the labels on foods can help people decide which foods should be avoided, or at least eaten in smaller amounts or less often.

Salt and blood pressure

High blood pressure, or **hypertension**, is a serious problem. More than 73 million Americans age 20 and older—or 1 in 3 adults—has high blood pressure. It affects close to 1 billion people worldwide. Most health professionals agree that reducing salt intake can lower blood pressure and cut the risk of heart disease or stroke.

Sports diets

While some young adults make unhealthy food choices, others are very careful about what they eat. Athletes reach their peak performance in young adulthood, and nutrition is a big part of their preparation.

The more we exercise, the more energy we need—and this energy comes from food, particularly carbohydrates. For people involved in competitive sports, carbohydrate-rich foods such as whole-grain pasta, potatoes, rice, oatmeal, and other cereals are a good source of energy.

Carbohydrates

The body produces energy from food by the process of **respiration**. The normal form of respiration requires oxygen, which people get by breathing. During digestion, the body breaks down complex carbohydrates to **glucose** for immediate energy use. Otherwise, it is stored in the muscles and liver as **glycogen**, to be used when needed. In the early stages of moderate exercise, up to half of the body's energy requirements come from carbohydrates.

Carbohydrates produce more energy per unit of oxygen than fats. During exercise, glycogen is converted back to glucose and is used for energy. The ability to maintain vigorous exercise over a long period depends on how much glycogen is stored in the muscles.

For a sports event lasting around 90 minutes, the glycogen stored in the muscles is generally enough to supply the energy required. For events lasting longer, such as a marathon run, athletes will consume a high-carbohydrate diet for the few days leading up to it. This maximizes the amount of glycogen stored in the muscles.

Complex carbohydrates

Complex carbohydrates come from "starchy" foods such as pasta, potatoes, and cereals. Simple carbohydrates are sugars, found in cookies, candy, and soft drinks. Complex carbohydrates provide more sustained energy than simple carbohydrates, as they are slowly broken down by the body to provide a steady supply of sugar over a longer period of time.

Calorie burning

Sports science laboratories measure how much energy is used and how fast an athlete uses it during exercise.

Fats

In a sports event lasting more than an hour, the body may get most of its energy from fats. Trained athletes use fat for energy more quickly than other people. For an endurance athlete, as much as 75 percent of the energy used may come from burning fat. Perhaps this is why we do not see many overweight marathon runners!

Protein

Muscle building is done by exercise and training, not by consuming large amounts of protein. An athlete's need for protein may increase, depending on the type of exercise and how often it is carried out, but a normal, varied diet should provide more than enough protein.

High-protein diets can actually lead to dehydration as they increase the amount of urine produced as the kidneys rid the body of poisonous wastes produced by breaking down proteins. The amounts of protein needed in the diet can vary according to the particular sport and it is always best to consult a qualified sports nutritionist for accurate advice.

Vitamins and minerals

There is no evidence that taking vitamins in the form of supplements will improve sports performance.

Athletes should get their vitamins and minerals from foods:

- B vitamins are needed to produce energy from food. Enough can be obtained from a well-balanced diet.

- Athletes put a lot of stress on their bones, and fractures are more likely to occur if there is insufficient calcium in the diet. Dairy products are the best source of calcium.

- Iron is an important part of red blood cells, which are responsible for transporting oxygen around the body. An adequate supply of iron is essential for endurance athletes. Lean red meat, dark poultry meat, whole grains, peas, and beans are all good sources of iron. Female athletes may need iron supplements to make up for losses from menstruation.

- Zinc is involved in the processes that produce energy in the body. It is also essential for making proteins and plays a part in the immune system. Zinc can be obtained from meat, poultry, seafood, and whole grains.

Water

Water provides zero calories and supplies none of the vitamins, minerals, or other nutrients we need. Yet it is an essential part of a healthy diet. Getting enough water every day is essential for our well-being.

Healthy hydration
It is important to replace the water we lose through sweat during exercise or on a hot day.

Essential water

The remarkable properties of water are essential for bodies to work:

- Water is a solvent: It can readily dissolve many substances, such as salts and sugars, and transport them around the body, plus all chemical reactions in cells take place in water.

- Water shapes **enzymes**: Enzymes are a type of protein that change the speed of chemical reactions in the body. In order to work, they have to be just the right shape. Water makes sure that they are.

- Water absorbs heat: Cells release a great deal of heat as a result of all of the chemical reactions going on in them. If it were not for water's ability to absorb heat energy, our cells would cook themselves.

- Some things don't like water: Some substances, such as oils, are repelled by water. The structure of our body's cells depends on this property of water.

Sources of water

Our bodies obtain water from three different sources:

- Drinking: We drink either plain water or water in the form of fruit juices, tea, coffee, soda, and so on.

- Food: Some fruits and vegetables contain a lot of water, but all foods have at least some.

- Respiration: The process of breaking down food to release energy produces water as a by-product (this is called **metabolic water**).

AMAZING BUT TRUE!

How much water are we?

A newborn baby is about 78 percent water. By the age of one, this has dropped to about 65 percent. About 60 percent of an adult male's body is water. Fat tissue does not have as much water as lean tissue, so overweight men have less water than thin men. Fat makes up more of the body in women than in men, so about 55 percent of their bodies are made of water.

How much water do we need?

The average healthy human body needs around half a gallon (2 liters) of water a day to replace what is lost in sweat and waste management. This has led to the belief, held by many people, that they have to drink half a gallon of fresh water a day to be healthy. This is simply a myth and not backed by science. Water obtained from drinking a cup of tea is as good as plain water for the body's needs, as is water obtained from food. Even something as seemingly dry as a baked potato can be 70 percent water. The amount of metabolic water produced in a day can be about 14 ounces (0.4 liters).

The human body is very good at maintaining its water balance. If it is in need of more water, it will trigger your feelings of thirst, and if you drink too much, you will soon find yourself running to the bathroom to get rid of it!

Growing Older

As we grow older the health consequences of our diet and lifestyle become more and more apparent. Poor nutrition means having to live with poor health, such as tooth decay and diabetes.

Tooth decay

One of the most common results of a poor diet is dental caries, or tooth decay. One of the causes of this can be an excess of sugary foods.

The enamel that covers our teeth is the hardest substance in the body, but it is vulnerable to attack by acids. Some drinks, such as orange juice, grapefruit juice, and colas, are acidic and can erode the enamel on teeth. A survey carried out in the United States found that 95 percent of people over the age of 50 had at least some evidence of tooth decay.

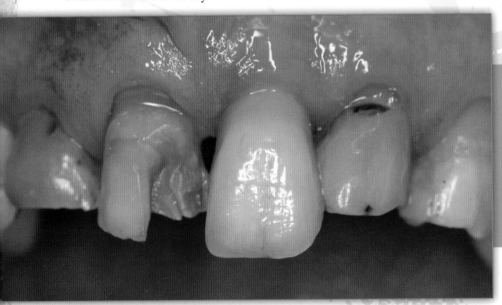

Tooth trouble

Tooth decay, caused by poor diet and a lack of dental hygiene, is one of the most common, and one of the most easily prevented, types of diseases.

Plaque attack

The biggest problem for teeth is **plaque**. This is a sticky deposit of food debris, saliva (spit), and bacteria that can collect on the teeth, particularly around the gum line. The bacteria in plaque turn sugars into lactic acid, which erodes (wears away) enamel.

A diet rich in sugars is simply providing a feast for the plaque bacteria. Sweet foods do not need to be avoided altogether, but they should be eaten in moderation and not snacked on throughout the day. (Remember that empty calories can cause weight gain, too.) Good dental hygiene, with regular tooth-brushing and visits to the dentist, is also important.

Diabetes and diet

Diabetes is a condition in which the body is unable to use glucose effectively. Type 1 diabetes is a result of problems with the immune system. The immune system attacks the cells in the pancreas that produce insulin, the chemical that lets our cells use glucose. Type 2 diabetes arises when the body does not make enough insulin or the insulin does not work properly. Between 90 and 95 percent of diabetics are type 2.

Monitoring diabetes
Testing for blood sugar levels at a clinic is a very simple procedure in the monitoring of diabetes.

Nutrition and cancer prevention

There is some evidence to suggest that a diet rich in fruits and vegetables may have a protective effect against some forms of cancer. Researchers have been looking into links between compounds in tomatoes and prostate cancer, for example. The American Cancer Society's nutrition guidelines recommend eating a balanced diet that includes a variety of fruits, vegetables, nuts, seeds, whole grains, and beans. Eating a wide variety of foods is likely to be healthier than large amounts of one type of food.

In some developing countries where many people have switched to high-energy "Western" foods, type 2 diabetes has become almost an epidemic. Once known as adult-onset diabetes, because it typically starts in adulthood, type 2 diabetes is now also found in adolescents and children. People who are overweight are at risk of developing type 2 diabetes. Fat deposits in the pancreas prevent it from releasing insulin effectively.

Heart disease and diet

Heart disease is the leading cause of death in many countries, including the United States. There are many causes of heart disease. Age is one of them. Men older than 45 and women older than 55 are at greater risk of heart disease. While age is beyond people's control, one of the most important risk factors can be easily controlled—diet.

Types of fat

There are two main types of fat: saturated and unsaturated. Foods containing saturated fats should be avoided in the diet, because these can raise cholesterol levels and lead to the formation of plaques (see page 39). Foods high in saturated fat include:

- butter
- cream
- hard cheeses
- lard
- sausages, bacon, and fatty cuts of meat
- cakes and cookies
- foods that contain coconut or palm oil

Small amounts of unsaturated fat will help reduce cholesterol levels and should be included in a balanced diet. Foods high in unsaturated fat include:

- nuts and seeds
- oily fish
- olive oil, sunflower oil, and other vegetable oils such as canola oil

Risk factors

There are several risk factors for heart disease. Some, such as age and gender, are out of our control, but others, such as the type of foods we eat and how much alcohol we drink, are lifestyle choices we can change.

Hardening of the arteries

Heart disease begins with a condition called atherosclerosis, or hardening of the **arteries**. Atherosclerosis occurs when substances such as fats and cholesterol build up in the walls of the arteries, forming hard substances called plaques. This makes the arteries narrower and stiffer, so blood does not flow through them as easily. Smaller blood vessels may be blocked completely. Some people with atherosclerosis may show no symptoms until they actually have a heart attack.

Thrombosis

A thrombosis is a blood clot inside a blood vessel. Thrombosis in an artery is usually associated with atherosclerosis. A heart attack is what happens when a thrombosis blocks an artery leading to the heart.

Preventing heart problems

A healthy diet is a good way to help reduce the risks of heart disease. A low-fat, high-fiber diet that includes whole grains and plenty of fresh fruits and vegetables is recommended by doctors. Limiting the amount of salt in the diet is also advised, because of the links with salt intake and high blood pressure (see page 31).

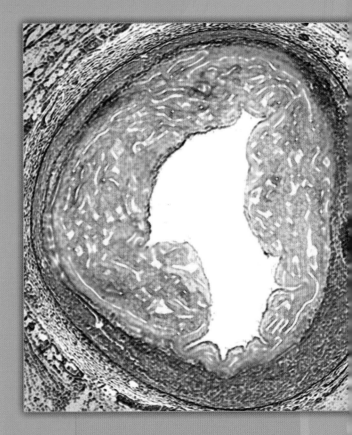

Blocked arteries
This magnified cross section of an artery shows how a build-up of fats reduces its volume, and so restricts the flow of blood through it.

Heart attack symptoms

The following are symptoms of a heart attack:

- a dull pain, ache, or "heavy" feeling in the chest
- a mild discomfort in the chest, similar to feelings of indigestion, that makes the person feel generally unwell
- pain or discomfort spreads to the arms, neck, jaw, back, or stomach
- feeling light-headed or dizzy and short of breath
- feeling nauseous or vomiting

If you suspect that someone is having a heart attack, you should call 911 immediately.

Therapeutic diets

Sometimes people may be advised to change their diet in order to treat or prevent disease. A diet that is used to help people suffering from health problems is called a therapeutic diet. One of the most obvious examples is a low-calorie diet for people who are obese.

Liver disease and diet

Among other things, the liver is a storehouse of energy, holding the body's reserves of glycogen. This is released to provide a steady source of energy between meals. If the liver is damaged, we lose this glycogen store. The body has to find other sources of energy and may begin to break down muscle and fat tissue.

People with liver disease may need to increase the amount of carbohydrates in their diet. Complex carbohydrates are an excellent slow-release source of energy. Including starchy foods like rice and potatoes at meals can help offset the lack of energy from the liver's glycogen store.

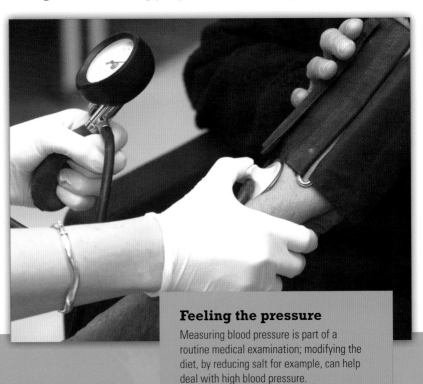

Feeling the pressure
Measuring blood pressure is part of a routine medical examination; modifying the diet, by reducing salt for example, can help deal with high blood pressure.

The DASH plan

DASH—dietary approaches to stop hypertension—is a diet that has been formulated to help people with high blood pressure (hypertension). Research studies by the U.S. National Heart, Lung, and Blood Institute to look into the effects of diet on hypertension found that the DASH plan was effective in lowering blood pressure.

The DASH diet has less salt and sodium, sugars, fats, and red meats than the typical Western diet. It is also high in fiber and lower in saturated fats and cholesterol and rich in nutrients that have been associated with lowering blood pressure such as potassium, magnesium, and calcium. This chart shows the basics of the DASH diet:

Eat	Avoid
Fruits and vegetables	Saturated fats
Fish and poultry	Foods with added sugars and sugary drinks
Fat-free or low-fat milk and milk products	Red meat
Whole grains, beans, seeds, and nuts	

Dialysis diet

The kidneys are the organs of the body that deal with the disposal of waste products from digestion, such as urea, and in regulating the amount of sodium and other substances in the blood. If the kidneys are not working properly, people may have to use a kidney dialysis machine to clear waste products from their blood.

But diet can also help. The dialysis diet is aimed at limiting the amount of food waste that builds up in the blood, particularly sodium, phosphorous, and potassium. Intake of foods that are high in sodium, such as salty snacks, canned soups, and fast foods, should be reduced. Meat and dairy products are high in phosphorous, and some fruits and vegetables have high amounts of potassium. People need to be careful about the amounts of these foods that are eaten.

Foods to be avoided

For example, bananas are high in potassium, and chips are high in sodium.

Foods that should be eaten

Adjusting diet

People with kidney disease are encouraged to eat certain foods and avoid others as much as possible.

Dietary supplements

Many people of all ages take dietary supplements of one sort or another, such as multivitamins, hoping to improve their health by doing so. But do these supplements actually do people any good? Could excessive amounts of these supplements actually be harmful?

What is a dietary supplement?

Dietary supplements, or nutritional supplements, are products that may contain vitamins, minerals, plant products (herbal remedies), enzymes, amino acids, or other substances that can also be found naturally in the foods we eat. They can come in the form of pills, capsules, powders, or liquids.

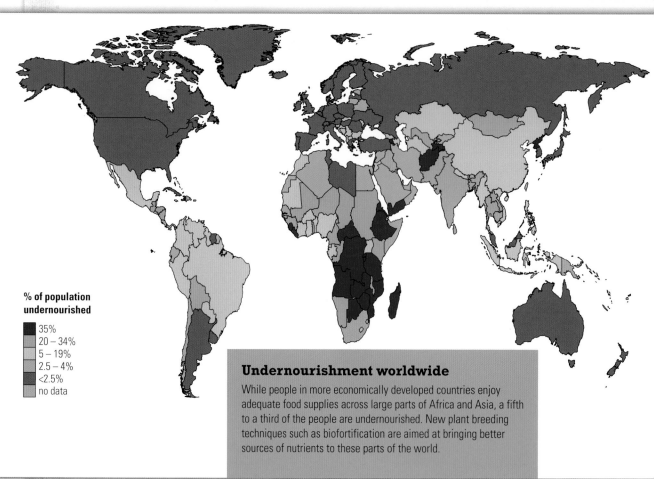

% of population undernourished

- 35%
- 20 – 34%
- 5 – 19%
- 2.5 – 4%
- <2.5%
- no data

Undernourishment worldwide

While people in more economically developed countries enjoy adequate food supplies across large parts of Africa and Asia, a fifth to a third of the people are undernourished. New plant breeding techniques such as biofortification are aimed at bringing better sources of nutrients to these parts of the world.

Biofortification

In many parts of the world, people subsist on a diet that does not always contain enough of the nutrients they need for good health, such as vitamin A, iron, and zinc. (The map shows what countries and regions are most severely affected.) A new type of plant breeding called biofortification may help to change this problem. Crossing wild varieties that are richer in nutrients with the crops normally grown is producing new varieties of food crops. The first crop to be produced in this way was a sweet potato, a staple food in many parts of Africa, that is far richer in vitamin A than normal varieties.

It could be argued that, if we have a good, balanced diet, we should be able to get all the nutrients we need from our food without turning to supplements. Most health care professionals would agree that supplements should not be used as a substitute for healthy eating. Vitamin C and the B vitamins are not stored in the body. If you take more than you need in the form of supplements, the body simply gets rid of the excess in urine.

However, there is evidence that supplements do have a role to play in some circumstances. For example, pregnant woman can benefit from additional iron (used in making red blood cells) and folic acid (essential for the development of the baby's brain and spinal cord). Many doctors also recommend that children between the ages of six months and five years have supplements of vitamins A, C, and D, as their diet may not be varied enough to ensure an adequate supply. Also, older women are often put on calcium supplements to prevent osteoporosis (see page 49).

No substitute for food
There is a danger that some people might use vitamin pills and other supplements as a substitute for a healthy, balanced diet of nutritious food.

Are supplements safe?

Many supplements contain ingredients such as caffeine that can have strong effects on the body. If people take supplements instead of prescribed medicines, or different supplements in combination, they may have unforeseen, harmful side effects. Some supplements have been shown to affect a person's response to the anesthetics used during surgery.

Often the food we eat (many breakfast cereals for example) has already been supplemented (fortified) with additional vitamins and minerals. If you take additional supplements you may actually be getting more than is good for your health. Too much vitamin A, for example, can damage the liver, reduce bone strength, and, if taken during pregnancy, can cause serious birth defects.

Too good to be true?

Sometimes supplements may make impressive sounding claims about things such as improving the memory, keeping joints supple, or boosting the immune system. It is important to look carefully at how these claims are worded. If a supplement says only that it may help with body maintenance ("helps maintain healthy joints"), but not that it will treat a medical condition ("will cure joint stiffness"), it will not be regulated in the same way as a medicine. It will not have been subjected to the same rigorous testing as a medicine and any evidence for its effects may not be conclusive.

Later Life

For most people in developed countries, at least, life at age 70 and beyond can continue to be fulfilling and enjoyable. Most people have access to good health care, and regular, gentle exercise and a varied, balanced diet will help to ensure continued good health.

Guidelines for later life

While the need for a balanced diet continues on into old age, the dietary requirements of an older person vary in some ways from those of a younger person:

- *A varied diet*: Older people generally need less energy than more active younger people, but fewer calories should not mean fewer nutrients. An older person needs nutrients just as much as a younger person, so it is important to keep the diet varied. The older person may be able to reduce quantities but should not skip key ingredients.

Senior nutrition

Older people should have a diet that includes plenty of fruits and vegetables, to ensure a good supply of vitamins and minerals.

Food and drinks high in fat/sugar—some fat is needed in the diet but should be eaten sparingly

Bread, rice, potatoes, pasta, and other starchy foods for carbohydrates, fiber, and vitamins

Meat, fish, eggs, pulses for protein, minerals, and vitamins

Milk and dairy foods for calcium, protein, and vitamins

Fruit and vegetables for vitamins, minerals, and fiber

- *Weight watching*: Being overweight puts a strain on bones that may be weakened by osteoporosis (see page 49). It also means the heart and lungs have to work harder at a time when they are becoming less efficient. Regular exercise is more effective at controlling weight than reducing food consumption.

- *Foods with fiber*: An older person's digestive system is less efficient at moving food along, and constipation (difficulty having bowel movements) can be a problem for the elderly. Plenty of fiber in the diet from fruits, vegetables, and whole-grain breads and cereals can help with this.

- *Get calcium*: Older women in particular should make sure their diet contains plenty of calcium, as this can help prevent the effects of osteoporosis.

- *Cut out empty calories*: Although it also provides some vitamins, fat provides more empty calories than any other food. It can also raise cholesterol levels, risking heart disease, so older people should limit empty calories.

- *Be careful with alcohol*: Overuse of alcohol can cause health problems for the elderly, just as it can for other ages. For example, it can accelerate the effects of osteoporosis and increase the likelihood of liver disease.

Senior malnutrition

Elderly people may not have an adequate balanced diet for a number of reasons. This may lead to malnutrition. Relatives and caregivers of the elderly need to be on the lookout for possible signs that an older person may not be eating properly, including:

- *Illness*: Decreased appetite can result from chronic illness or the side effects of medications. Memory loss and **dementia** (a decline in mental function) can lead to older people forgetting to eat.

- *Depression*: The loss of loved ones, failing health, and reduced mobility can all lead to depression, with a consequent loss of interest in food.

- *Diet restrictions*: People advised to cut out certain foods for medical reasons might end up not getting sufficient nutrients if their intake is not carefully monitored.

- *Limited income*: Many older people may cut down on their food budget when trying to save money.

Eating alone

Many older people live alone and may not feel motivated to cook proper meals for themselves.

Muscle and metabolism

As we grow older, the body's muscle mass decreases and strength is reduced. Fat is deposited in muscle tissues, and the muscle fibers shrink. Muscle tissue is replaced much more slowly as we age. This can be seen, for example, in the hands of an elderly person, which may appear thin and bony. Although muscle changes are thought of as part of growing old, they may actually begin in men in their twenties and women in their forties. By the age of 40, adults are losing between 0.5 and 2 percent of their muscle mass each year.

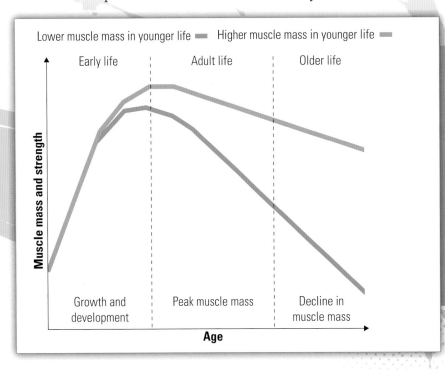

Lower muscle mass in younger life ▬ Higher muscle mass in younger life ▬

Early life | Adult life | Older life

Muscle mass and strength

Growth and development | Peak muscle mass | Decline in muscle mass

Age

Muscle mass changes

Research has discovered that the decline in muscle mass in the elderly may be linked to the peak of muscle mass reached in earlier life. Those people with a higher muscle mass in younger life are more likely to lose it at a lower rate than those with less muscle mass.

One of the most important results of losing muscle mass is a decline in the body's metabolic rate. This may lead to obesity if people are not careful to adjust the body's energy balance. This can be done by a combination of reducing calories and increasing the amount of exercise, if possible.

Changing needs

The body's need for calories changes as we grow older, and the amount of body fat increases as muscle mass decreases. Older people are generally less active, which also reduces the calorie requirement. Elderly people have to ensure that their diet still has an adequate nutrient content, while cutting calories.

Choosing foods that are "nutrient dense" is important. These foods have high nutritional value and low calorie value. Low-fat milk, for example, has the same nutrients as high-fat milk, but it has fewer calories because of the reduction in fat, so it is more nutrient dense. Reducing fat in the diet is the simplest way to cut calories.

Reversing the trend

The body is continually breaking down old proteins and replacing them with new ones. Immediately after a meal, the body starts building new proteins from the raw materials that the food makes available to it. At the same time, the rate at which older proteins are being broken down decreases. This means that there is a net gain in protein. In older people, the rate at which proteins are broken down does not slow to the same extent. The result is that more protein is lost, which means an increase in muscle loss.

Loss of muscle mass is a major problem for the elderly, as it can leave them unable to carry out many normal activities. However, researchers have discovered that the trend may be reversed by exercise and training. In a study in Canada, 25 healthy, active elderly people (with an average age of 70) and an equal number of college students (with an average age of 26) were given a program of weight training exercises. At the start, the younger people were, unsurprisingly, much stronger than the elderly group, who were 59 percent weaker than the students. After six months of training, however, the gap had been lessened, and the older people were just 38 percent weaker.

Exercise for life
The loss of muscle mass in later life can be reversed by a combination of regular exercise and a healthy diet.

Old bones

Your bones are as much a part of your living body as any other organ. Like the rest of your body, they are being maintained all the time using nutrients from the food you eat. One important role the bones play is as a store for calcium. Among other things, calcium plays a part in regulating blood pressure and in nerve and muscle activity. It is important to have a good supply of calcium in the diet.

Calcium

Throughout childhood, adolescence, and early adulthood, large amounts of calcium and other substances are being added to the bone as the skeleton develops and strengthens. The body cannot make calcium itself, so all our calcium needs must come from our diet. Good sources of calcium include dairy products such as milk and cheese, vegetables such as cabbage, brussels sprouts, and broccoli, and nuts such as almonds.

Mass reduction

Up until the age of about 30 to 35, new bone mass is being formed in the body at a faster rate than old bone material is broken down. The result of this is that the amount of bone mass increases until it reaches a peak at around this age. Beyond this point, the breakdown of old bones starts to happen faster than new bone is being produced. This means that bone mass now gradually decreases. The amount of calcium in the bone also decreases.

In women, bone loss is faster in the first five years after menopause, when the menstrual cycle ceases and women can no longer have children. This is because production of the hormone estrogen, which influences bone formation, stops at this time.

Bone gain and loss

As this graph shows, from around the age of 35 or so the amount of bone in our bodies decreases. For women, there is a sharp decline during and after menopause.

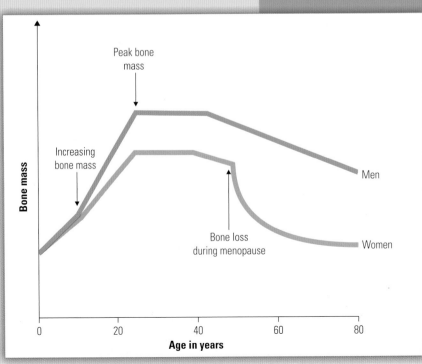

The amount of calcium the body needs rises steadily from about 270 milligrams a day at six months to 1,300 milligrams a day between 14 and 18 years old. After that, when most bone growth is completed, the amount needed declines.

Vitamin D

Vitamin D is also important for healthy bones, because it helps the body to absorb calcium. Vitamin D is made by the action of sunlight on the skin, and about 90 percent of the body's vitamin D needs can be met in this way. Vitamin D deficiency may result in a condition known as rickets, in which the sufferer feels pains in the bones and the joints may become enlarged. A lack of vitamin D can be a problem for housebound elderly people.

Osteoporosis

If large amounts of bone tissue are lost, the bones can become weak, brittle, and able to break easily. This condition is called osteoporosis. All bones can be affected by osteoporosis, but fractures are most common in the wrist, spine, and hip. Fractures to the spine are what cause the hunched appearance of some older people. Osteoporosis does not just affect older people. It can also have an effect on younger men and women who have had an eating disorder.

Osteoporosis is a condition that is easier to prevent than to cure. Regular exercise and a good diet in early life will help to ensure healthy bones in later years. Tests in which women were given calcium tablets to strengthen their bones showed an increase in bone mass of only 1 or 2 percent.

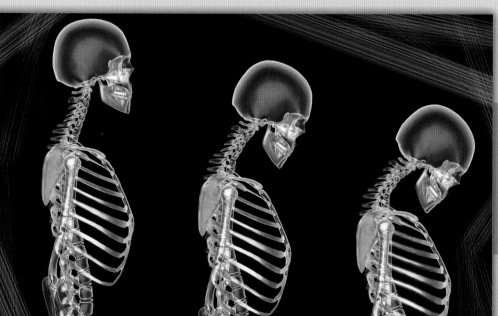

Curving spine
One effect of osteoporosis can be a curvature of the spine, leading to the stooped appearance of some elderly people.

Nutrients and aging

A problem in old age can be the body's reduced ability to absorb nutrients such as proteins, vitamins, and minerals. Illnesses are also much more likely as we get older, and these can reduce the body's stores of vitamins. Some medications can also affect the body's ability to utilize nutrients. A good, varied diet is essential to make sure the body's requirements are met.

Vitamin maintenance

The need for vitamins remains high as we grow older, even as the need for calories declines. Vitamins A, D, E, and K are not needed by the body every day and can be stored in the liver until required. Elderly people are at low risk of running short of these vitamins. Drinking milk fortified with vitamin D can ensure that housebound elderly people and others who are prevented from getting enough sunlight get enough of this vitamin.

Vitamin E and Alzheimer's disease

Claims have been made that eating foods rich in vitamin E, such as whole grains, peanuts, nuts, and seeds, may help to reduce the risk of Alzheimer's disease, a condition that results in loss of memory, dementia, and personality changes. There is some evidence that suggests that vitamin E helps to prevent damage to brain cells, but it is inconclusive. Too much vitamin E taken in supplements has actually been linked with an increased risk of heart failure.

Different needs

Although people have different nutritional requirements depending on their age, a balanced diet with a wide variety of foods is a great idea for everyone.

B vitamins and vitamin C are not stored by the body, so it is essential that these are supplied in the diet on a daily basis. Vitamin C improves the body's absorption of iron, a nutrient that is often low in the elderly. Low levels of vitamin B12 have been associated with memory loss and hearing loss in older adults. Folic acid (vitamin B9) may actually improve hearing, but high folic acid levels may cause health concerns if levels of B12 are low. As we age, our ability to absorb vitamin B12 decreases. Older people are advised to eat foods rich in vitamin B12, such as meat, poultry, fish, eggs, and dairy foods, as a regular part of their diet.

Think zinc

Zinc is an essential part of the diet. It is involved in the process of wound healing and in the senses of vision, taste, and smell. Elderly people can sometimes have low zinc levels, especially if their diet is restricted. The body more readily absorbs zinc from animal foods, such as red meat, fish, and poultry, than it does zinc from plant foods. The best sources of zinc are red meats, poultry, cheese, and shellfish, particularly oysters. Beans, peas, sunflower seeds, and peanuts are also good sources. The need for zinc is a good example of the importance of eating a balanced diet with a wide variety of foods.

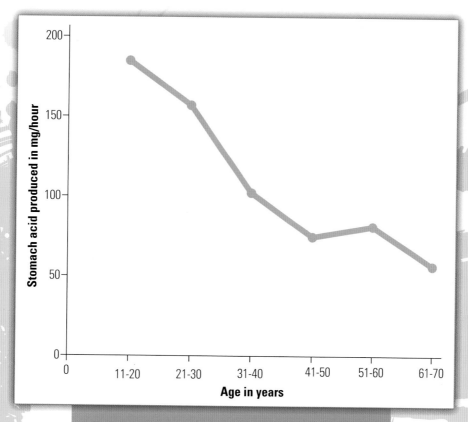

Stomach acid

As we grow older, the amount of acid produced by the stomach declines. This means that proteins are not digested as efficiently as before. Essential minerals such as calcium, iron, and zinc are also not absorbed as well when stomach acid is low.

Food and senses

As we grow older, our senses change and deteriorate. This can have an effect on the way older people approach food and nutrition.

As we age, our sense of taste changes. Sensitivity to salt and bitter tastes declines first. This can lead to older people over-salting their food to compensate, possibly resulting in an unhealthy amount of salt in their diet. At the same time, the taste for sweet foods stays well developed, which may lead to over-indulging in foods like cakes and sugary snacks.

Our sense of sight also has a role to play in nutrition. A well-presented, colorful plate of food can look enticing and stimulate the appetite. If elderly people cannot clearly see what they are eating, this is another factor that may discourage them from eating properly.

Poor sight can have other consequences, too. It makes it hard to read food labels and recipes, so elderly people are less likely to plan their meals as carefully as they would have when they were younger. A combination of poor sight and the loss of coordination that can come with aging can result in the elderly stopping cooking for themselves, as they fear accidents in the kitchen.

Sense and appetite

Taste and smell are an important part of the way our bodies respond to food. Signals sent from these sense organs trigger the body to start releasing digestive fluids from the salivary glands, the stomach, and the pancreas. These all prepare the way for the body to digest the food we are about to eat.

The sense of taste enables us to choose between different foods according to the body's nutritional requirements at the time. Experiments have shown that taste detectors can become more sensitive to certain minerals that are lacking in the diet. Our senses of taste and smell give us an indication of how nutritious the food we eat is likely to be. They play a big part in the quantity of food we eat, so it can be a concern when taste and smell decline in the elderly.

AMAZING BUT TRUE!

Fantastic flavor

There is more to the flavor of a food than just its taste. Flavor is a combination of taste, smell, and feel. Smell, in particular, helps us to decide what type of food it is we are eating. Most people can identify around 1,000 different odors, and people who trained their sense, such as perfumers, can identify 10 times as many. The sense of touch tells us how food feels in the mouth, and other sensors respond to chemicals such as those that make mint feel cool and peppers feel hot!

Tasty explorations

Not being able to appreciate a plate of food as fully as before can result in older people losing interest in eating and not getting the nutrients they need. Elderly people should be encouraged to be adventurous with their eating. Trying out new flavors and experimenting with seasonings can revitalize their desire to eat. Food that does not smell or taste enticing is not likely to be eaten.

Finding new and interesting things to eat isn't just good for the body. It can be good for the mind too. Looking for recipes to try out, visiting markets to find ingredients and sharing ideas with friends are great ways to make life more enjoyable, and healthy too.

Experiment and enjoy
People of any age can enjoy the process of cooking a meal. And experimenting with new dishes and flavors is a great way to maintain a varied, healthy, and fun diet.

The end of life

At some point, people who are terminally ill may no longer be capable of feeding themselves—or even of letting others know that they are hungry or thirsty. Just how much nutrition they actually require may be open to question, however.

Shutting down

When a person is terminally ill and approaching the end of life, the normal functions of the body begin to shut down. As these functions include those of the digestive system the body can no longer deal with food and fluids as it could when the person was fully healthy.

Decreased blood flow causes a drop in the production of saliva from the salivary glands and slows down the release of digestive enzymes. The result is that the digestive system operates much more slowly. The dying person begins to lose weight and becomes lethargic.

In one study, doctors carefully observed terminally ill cancer patients over the last year of their lives. Of the 32 patients monitored during the study, 20 never experienced any hunger. Similarly, 20 experienced either no thirst or thirst only at the beginning of the time they were under observation. In all patients, giving small amounts of food and fluids, or applying ice chips to the lips, could ease symptoms of hunger, thirst, and dry mouth. The amount of fluid given was far less than would have been needed to prevent dehydration. Comfort care included the use of drugs for pain relief in most patients.

Ethical questions

How much nutrition actually needs to be given to terminally ill patients? Giving nutrition beyond what the patient wants may actually lead to discomfort. If a terminally ill patient cannot digest food properly it may cause nausea, vomiting, and other unpleasant effects. Instead, nutrients and water may have to be administered medically, raising ethical questions about prolonging life and the quality of life.

Considerations such as this have been challenging the wisdom of artificial nutrition for the terminally ill. Because one of the ways we care for each other is by giving food, it can be difficult for the family of a dying person to accept that artificial nutrition can do more harm than good.

Artificial nutrition

The decision to feed a dying person artificially is a difficult one. Artificial nutrition means supplying nutrients by means other than the person swallowing them. Nutrients may be delivered through a tube inserted into the digestive tract or by a smaller tube inserted into a vein. When these treatments were first developed, they were intended as temporary measures to be used to help a person who was expected to recover, and not as a means to prolong life indefinitely.

A ripe old age
A long life may be the reward for looking after our health and ensuring that our bodies are well nourished.

Food for life

We begin life as infants in immediate need of nourishment, and throughout life the care and attention we pay to nourishing our bodies plays a huge role in ensuring that we stay healthy for as long as possible. People in their nineties can regain muscle mass through exercise, improving their appetites and thus helping to ensure they get the nutrients they need. Understanding and meeting our nutritional needs helps us to live life longer and to the fullest.

Quiz

Find out how much you remember about the changing nutritional needs we have throughout our lives by completing this quiz. You will find the answers on page 63.

1. Which vitamin is produced naturally by the body when the skin is exposed to sunlight?
    a.) vitamin C   b.) vitamin D   c.) vitamin A   d.) vitamin B

2. How many people are estimated to die each year in the United States as a result of food allergies?
    a.) 50–100   b.) 150–200   c.) 500–600   d.) 1,000

3. According to figures published in 2008, how many children are obese in the United States?
    a.) 1 in 3   b.) 1 in 5   c.) 1 in 50   d.) 1 in 100

4. How much muscle mass do adults over age 40 lose each year?
    a.) 0.5–2 percent   b.) 1.2 percent   c.) 12 percent   d.) 15 percent

5. Approximately how many calories a day does the average adult need to maintain body weight?
    a.) 1,000   b.) 1,800   c.) 2,000   d.) 3,000

6. Your body can make all the calcium it needs.
    True or false?

7. The more protein you consume, the bigger your muscles will be.
    True or false?

8. Vegetarians have to take food supplements to get all the nutrients they need. True or false?

9. A 14-year-old boy can consume twice as many calories as an adult. True or false?

10. What foods are best avoided if you want to lower your risk of developing heart disease?

11. What is the recommended limit for salt in the diet?
a.) 1 gram per day   b.) 6 grams per day
c.) 16 grams per day   d.) 60 grams per day

12. Why is it not a good idea to give untreated cow's milk to a young baby?

13. During exercise, what happens to the glycogen stored in the muscles?

14. What sort of foods would you eat to obtain complex carbohydrates?

Facts and Figures

Nutrient deficiencies

The following statistics reflect the toll that nutrient deficiencies have worldwide:

- Worldwide, more than 500,000 child deaths every year are linked to a lack of vitamin A.

- More than 20 percent of children under five in developing countries suffer from iron deficiency–related anemia, which means that the body does not produce enough red blood cells.

- About 176,000 people die from diarrhea linked to zinc deficiency each year.

- About 178 million children are physically stunted, partly because of not having enough food or vitamins.

Calorie burning

How many calories are you using? The following list shows approximately how many calories are burned in different activities:

- *Riding a bike*: 118–172 calories per hour

- *Skateboarding*: 74–108 calories per hour

- *Ballet*: 71–103 calories per hour

- *Doing homework*: 27–39 calories per hour

- *Playing computer games*: 22–32 calories per hour

- *Watching television*: 15–22 calories per hour

- *Sleeping*: 13–19 calories per hour

Facts on food

The following are some interesting facts about food:

- Twelve plant species provide three-quarters of the world's food.

- Over half of the world's food energy comes from varieties of wheat, rice, and maize (corn).

- Around 330 million tons of meat are produced each year—at least 60 percent of it in developed countries.

- Seventeen percent of the world's cultivated land is used for growing wheat.

- Wheat is the staple food for 35 percent of the world's population.

- Ninety percent of the world's rice is grown and consumed in Asia.
- One million farmers in Latin America and the Caribbean depend on rice as their main source of income.
- Half of the world's maize is grown in Asia.
- In South Asia, most maize is used to feed humans.
- In East Asia, most maize is used to feed animals.

What people are eating

People around the world have very different diets.

The average American consumes the following each year:

- *Beef*: 58.1 pounds (26.35 kilograms)
- *Pork*: 46.6 pounds (21.14 kilograms)
- *Poultry*: 69.4 pounds (31.48 kilograms)
- *Eggs*: 246.1 pounds (111.6 kilograms)
- *Dairy products*: 607.1 pounds (275.4 kilograms)
- *Fats*: 78.6 pounds (35.7 kilograms)
- *Flour and cereal products*: 194.5 pounds (88.2 kilograms)

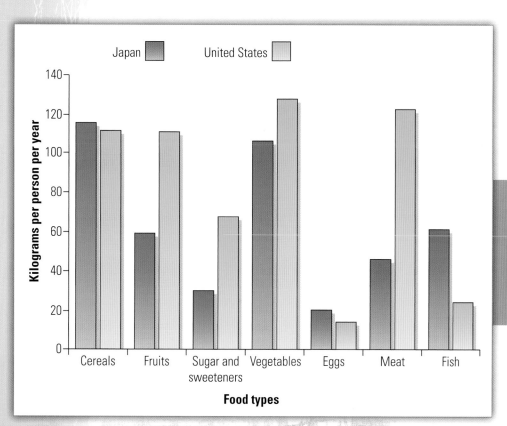

Country comparison

This chart shows the amounts of food eaten per person each year in Japan and the United States.

Glossary

adolescence period during which a person develops from a child into an adult

adolescent young person in the process of developing from a child into an adult

allergy response by the body's immune system to a harmless substance such as plant pollen or a particular food

appestat region of the brain that is believed to control the appetite for food

artery major blood vessel that carries oxygenated blood to the tissues of the body

calorie unit of energy, usually used to measure the energy present in food

carbohydrate one of the three main food groups, carbohydrates include starches and sugars and are a source of energy in the diet

cell smallest unit of life; we are made up of trillions of cells working together

chemical reaction process by which one or more substances are changed into one or more new substances

cholesterol waxy substance that is an essential part of all cells but which in some forms can block blood vessels

deficiency lack or shortage of something

dementia disorder of the mental processes resulting from damage to the brain caused by disease or injury

developed country country with relatively high living standards and technological development

developing country country with relatively low living standards and less reliance on industry and technology

diabetes disease in which a person has a high blood sugar level because the body does not produce enough insulin or does not respond well to it

digestive system body system that breaks down food to make the nutrients it contains available

enzyme type of substance produced by living things to regulate the speed of chemical reactions in cells; all enzymes are proteins

fat one of the three main food groups, fats include animal fats and vegetable oils. They are stored in the body as a source of energy.

fetus unborn baby

fiber indigestible part of plant food

folic acid vitamin B9, a vitamin that is essential for the growth of cells

glucose simplest form of sugar. The body's cells use glucose to obtain energy.

glycogen form in which the body stores glucose until it is needed

hypertension abnormally high blood pressure that can increase the risk of heart disease and may cause damage to the kidneys

immune system body system that works to protect it from disease

intolerance adverse reaction that occurs whenever a particular type of food is eaten

kilocalorie 1,000 calories

macronutrient substance required in relatively large amounts in the diet

malnutrition condition that results when nutrients are lacking in the diet

metabolic rate rate at which metabolism takes place. It is the amount of energy used up over a given period of time.

metabolic water water created inside a living thing as a by-product of metabolism

metabolism all of the chemical processes that go on inside a living thing to sustain life

micronutrient substance required in small quantities in the diet

mineral one of the chemical elements required by the body, such as calcium and zinc

nerve type of cell that transmits information from one part of the body to another

nervous system body system that gathers information about its surroundings and transmits information and instructions from one part of the body to another

nutrient substance that is needed in a balanced diet to ensure good health

nutritionist person who studies nutrition

obese very overweight

obesity medical condition in which body fat has accumulated to such a degree that it becomes a threat to health

osteoporosis condition in which the bones become fragile due to a loss of bone tissue

plaque deposit that forms on teeth made up of food fragments and bacteria

protein one of the three main food groups, proteins are a group of complex molecules formed by living things to carry out a number of tasks, including building cell structure and acting as an enzyme

respiration process by which energy is obtained from food by reacting oxygen with glucose

saturated fat type of fat found in foods such as butter, cream, and fatty meats that can raise the amounts of cholesterol in the blood

stroke disturbance in the blood supply to the brain, usually caused by a blood clot. A stroke can lead to the loss of mental and physical ability and even death.

supplement addition to something to make up a deficiency

tissue group of similar cells in the body working together to perform a particular task, such as muscle tissue or bone tissue

vitamin essential compound involved in a variety of processes in the body, vitamins are needed in small amounts in the diet for good health

weaning process of getting a child used to foods other than milk

Find Out More

Books

Ambrose, Marylou. *Investigating Diabetes: Real Facts for Real Lives* (*Investigating Diseases*). Berkeley Heights, N.J.: Enslow, 2010.

Burgan, Michael. *Making Food Choices* (*Ethics of Food*). Chicago: Heinemann Library, 2012.

Currie-McGhee, L. K. *Teenage Alcoholism* (*Compact Research*). San Diego: ReferencePoint, 2012.

D'Alusio, Faith. *What the World Eats*. Berkeley, Calif.: Tricycle, 2008.

Mayhew, Maggie. *How to Cook*. New York: Dorling Kindersley, 2011.

Miller, Debra. *Vegetarianism* (*Current Controversies*). Detroit: Greenhaven, 2010.

Morris, Neil. *Food Technology* (*Sci-Hi: Science and Technology*). Chicago: Raintree, 2012.

Smolin, Lori A., and Mary B. Grosvenor. *Nutrition for Sports and Exercise* (*Eating Right*). New York: Chelsea House, 2010.

Web sites

www.fda.gov/Food/ResourcesForYou/Consumers/ucm109760.htm
Find out about dietary supplements and their possible benefits at this U.S. Food and Drug Administration site.

www.nlm.nih.gov/medlineplus/alcohol.html
This guide, made by the U.S. National Library of Medicine, explains the potential dangers to health posed by alcohol.

kidshealth.org/kid/ill_injure/sick/food_allergies.html
Learn more about food allergies at this KidsHealth page.

kidshealth.org/kid/stay_healthy/food/sports.html#
Learn more about nutrition and sports at this KidsHealth page.

Places to visit

The Exploratorium
3601 Lyon Street
San Francisco, California 94123
www.exploratorium.edu
Learn all about the human body
at this museum.

The Health Museum
1515 Hermann Drive
Houston, Texas 77004
www.mhms.org
This museum offers interactive
exhibits about the body and health.

Topics to research

Here are some other topics you might like to research:

What did you eat today?
Do you eat a healthy diet? Try keeping a food diary for a month and find out exactly what you are eating. Be honest with your entries!

"Fresh" foods?
Where does the food we eat come from? How far has it traveled before it reaches our plates, and what has been done to preserve it?

A world of food
What sort of things do the peoples of different countries and cultures eat, and how do these things differ from what you eat? How many of the world's people actually enjoy a good, balanced diet?

Quiz answers (see pages 56–57)

1) b. About 90 percent of our vitamin D is produced by sunlight.

2) b.

3) b.

4) a.

5) c. The actual amount can vary depending on how active the individual is. An active male may need 3,000 calories a day, while an inactive female may need around 1,600.

6) False. All of our calcium needs come from our diet.

7) False. The body stores excess protein as fat.

8) False. A well-balanced vegetarian diet provides all the nutrients needed for good health.

9) True. This is a time of rapid growth.

10) Avoid foods high in saturated fats such as butter, cream, fatty meats, cakes, and cookies.

11) b.

12) One of the parts making up cow's milk can cause irritation and bleeding in the digestive tract of very young children.

13) The glycogen is converted to glucose, which is used to produce energy.

14) Complex carbohydrates come from starchy foods such as potatoes and cereals.

Index